Little Mitchie

WHY DO DOGS WAG THEIR TAILS?

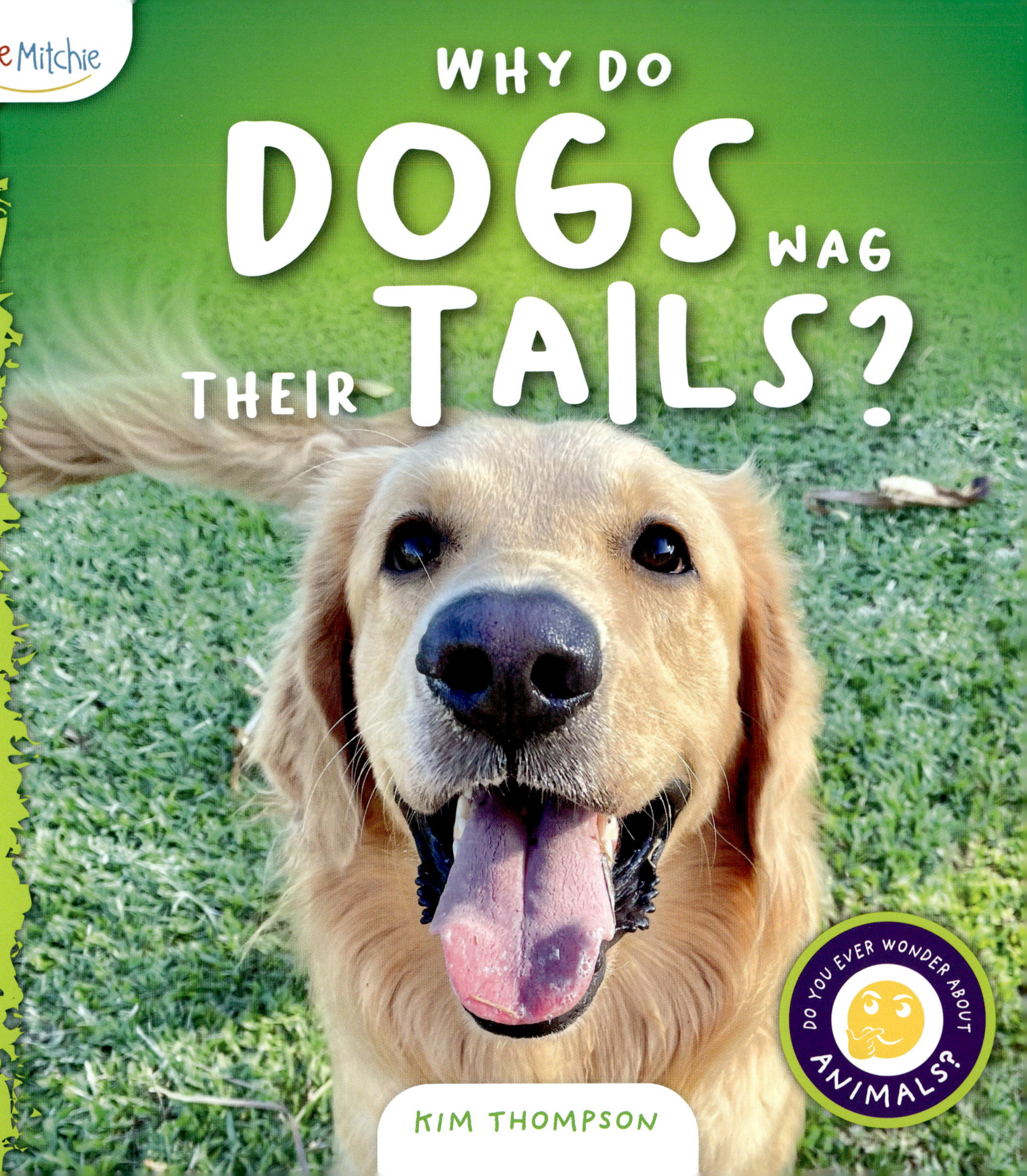

DO YOU EVER WONDER ABOUT ANIMALS?

KIM THOMPSON

CREATING YOUNG NONFICTION READERS

Little Mitchie books spark curiosity and support early nonfiction reading for students in Grades 2-3. Designed to build vocabulary, support second language learners, and prepare readers for middle-grade content, each book includes helpful tips for parents and educators to build confidence and deepen understanding of the world.

TIPS FOR READING NONFICTION WITH BEGINNING READERS

Talk about Nonfiction

Begin by explaining that nonfiction books give us information that is true. The book will be organized around a specific topic or idea, and we may learn new facts through reading.

Look at the Parts

Most nonfiction books have helpful features. Our *Little Mitchie* titles include color photographs and graphic aids, a table of contents, a glossary, and an index. Share the purpose of these features with your reader.

Color Photos and Graphic Aids

A lot of information can be found by "reading" photos, charts, maps, and other graphic aids found within nonfiction texts. Help your reader learn more about the different ways information can be displayed.

Table of Contents

Located at the front of the book, this list shows the big ideas within the text and the page numbers where they can be found.

Glossary

Located at the back of the book, the glossary defines key words and phrases that are related to the topic. These words and phrases can be found in the text in colored type.

Index

Located at the back of the book, an index is an alphabetical list of topics and the page numbers where they can be found.

With a little help and guidance about reading nonfiction, you can feel good about introducing a young reader to the world of *Little Mitchie* nonfiction books.

Little Mitchie is an imprint of:

Mitchell Lane
PUBLISHERS

2001 SW 31st Avenue
Hallandale, FL 33009
mitchelllanepub.com

First Edition, 2027.

Author: Kim Thompson
Designer: Jen Bowers

Library of Congress Cataloging-in-Publication Data
Title: Why Do Dogs Wag Their Tails? / by Kim Thompson

Description: Hallandale, FL :
Mitchell Lane Publishers, [2027]

Identifiers:
ISBN 979-8-89260-925-8 (library bound)
ISBN 979-8-89260-980-7 (eBook)

Library of Congress Control Number: 2026936355

PHOTO CREDITS
Shutterstock: cover, p.1, 22 ©2023 demibombe, p.5 ©2017 Kitreel, p.6 ©2018 Mary Swift, p.7 ©2021 Natalia Fedosova, p.9 ©2021 Jaromir Chalabala, p.10–11, 22 ©2024 Maian Vivier, p.13 ©2016 Veda Wildfire, p.14 ©2023 Kub The Shadow Simple Man, p.15 ©2016 CREATISTA , p.17 ©2016 BublikHaus, p.18 ©2024 sergey kolesnikov, p.19 ©2017 Porytska_M, p.21 ©2024 Sonja Schneider, p.22 ©2020 Peyker

TABLE OF CONTENTS

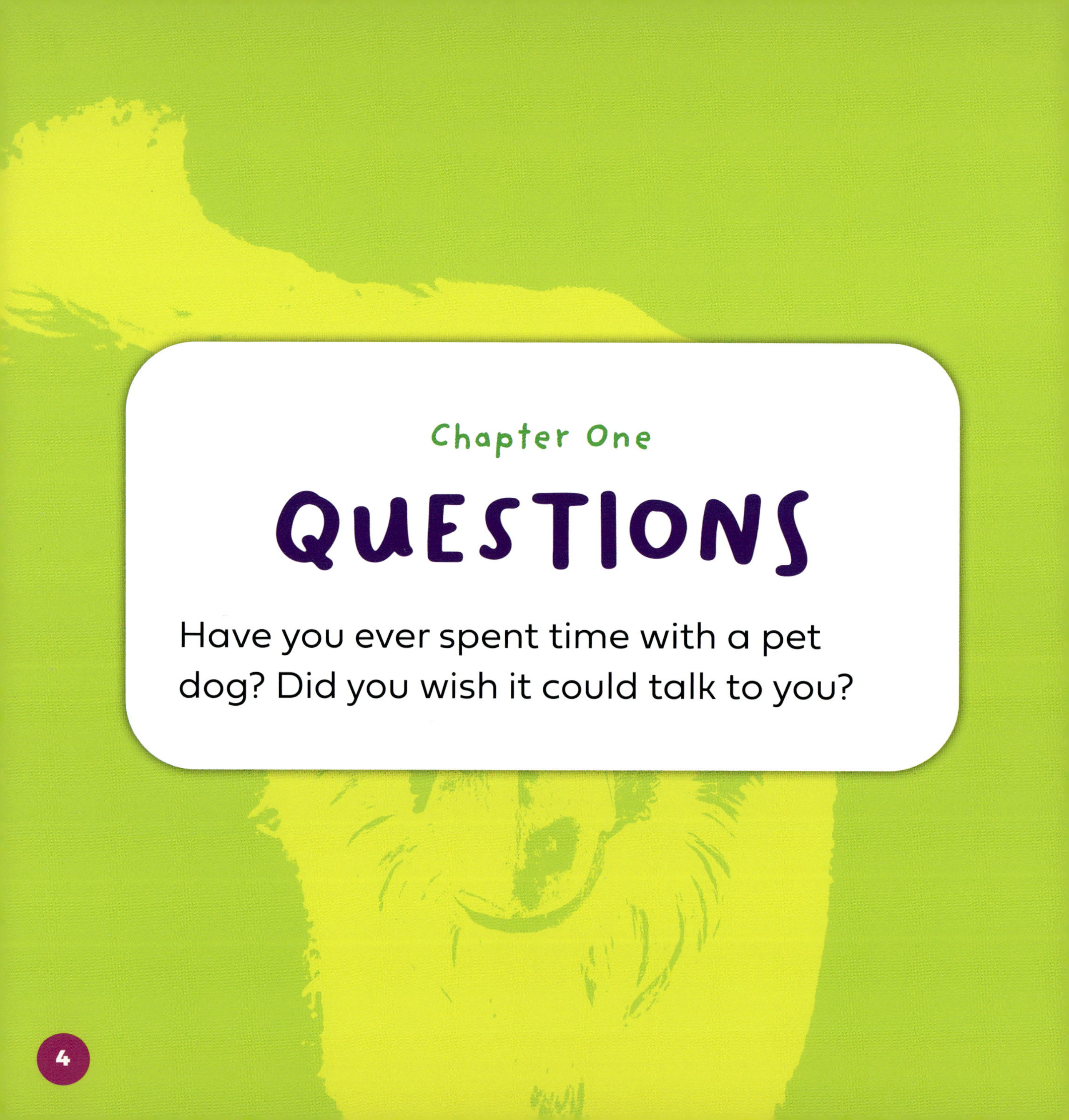

Chapter One

QUESTIONS

Have you ever spent time with a pet dog? Did you wish it could talk to you?

You probably wondered about dog **communication**. You may have asked these questions.

1. Why do dogs wag their tails?
2. What can you tell from a dog's face?
3. In what other ways do dogs send messages?

Chapter Two

WHAT KIND OF WAGGING?

Dogs are smart. They communicate in **complex** ways. The main way they show thoughts and feelings is through **body language**.

ANIMAL WONDER

Dogs can follow commands and do tricks. They are about as intelligent as a two-year-old child.

A wagging tail can mean different things. High, fast wagging shows excitement. Wagging in a circle can show happiness. Low, slow, or stiff wagging can mean that a dog feels **threatened**.

ANIMAL WONDER

Look at a dog's whole body to read its **mood**. A **crouching** dog may be afraid. A dog that looks like it is taking a bow is ready to play.

Chapter Three

FACING FACTS

You can tell a lot from a dog's face. If a dog blinks and looks at you with a soft **gaze**, it is relaxed. A dog with wide-open, staring eyes is ready to fight!

ANIMAL WONDER

Upright ears show that a dog is happy and **curious**. A scared dog flattens its ears and pulls them back.

A yawn could mean that a dog is bored. It may also signal stress.

Dogs lick to explore their world. They may lick you to show trust and **affection**.

Chapter Four

ACTING OUT

Dogs also communicate through their **behavior**. A dog that paws at you is asking for attention. It may want food, water, or comfort. It may want to play!

ANIMAL WONDER

Paying close attention to your dog helps you **interpret** its signals. It helps build trust between you and your pet.

What if a dog holds up a paw? Stands on its hind legs? It is saying, "Feed me!"

What if a dog rolls over? Rubs its head against you? The message is, "Please give me a scratch!"

Chapter Five

ANSWERS

Now, you can answer your questions.

1. **WHY DO DOGS WAG THEIR TAILS?**

   Dogs wag their tails in different ways to show different feelings.

2. **WHAT CAN YOU TELL FROM A DOG'S FACE?**

   You can tell many things, like whether the dog is relaxed, bored, or stressed.

3. **IN WHAT OTHER WAYS DO DOGS SEND MESSAGES?**

   Dogs communicate through behaviors such as rolling over and pawing.

ANIMAL WONDER

Keep asking questions about animals. That's how you learn about the amazing creatures that share our world!

DOG COMMUNICATION CHART

HAPPY
- Relaxed body
- Open mouth
- Wagging tail

WORRIED
- Tense body
- Low tail
- Licks lips or yawns
- Avoids eye contact

VERY STRESSED
- Very tense body
- May cower or shake
- May snarl and show teeth

GLOSSARY

affection (uh-FEK-shuhn) love and care

behavior (bi-HAYV-yur) the way an animal acts

body language (BAH-dee LANG-gwij) body movements used to show feelings and communicate with others

communication (kuh-myoo-ni-KAY-shuhn) sharing thoughts, feelings, and information with others

complex (kuhm-PLEKS) very complicated or highly developed

crouching (KROU-ching) bending to lower the body; hunched over

curious (KYOOR-ee-uhs) excited to know or learn about something

gaze (gayz) a look

interpret (in-TUR-prit) to figure out what something means

mood (mood) the way someone is feeling

threatened (THRET-uhnd) feeling scared or in danger

FURTHER READING

Mattice, Lindy. *How to Speak Animal: Decode the Secret Language of Dogs, Cats, Birds, Reptiles, and More!* Bushel and Peck Books, 2022.

Moore, Arden. *A Kid's Guide to Dogs: How to Train, Care for, and Play and Communicate with Your Amazing Pet!* Storey Publishing, 2020.

ON THE INTERNET

BBC Earth Kids: How Do Dogs Communicate?
youtube.com/watch?v=z3AV_7BtovQ&t=30s
Watch and interpret the body language of a cute and energetic puppy.

Mystery Science: Can My Pet Understand What I'm Saying?
youtube.com/watch?v=DQfTcPVN1C4
Learn how to communicate with your dog.

National Geographic Kids: 10 Awesome Dog Facts!
natgeokids.com/uk/discover/animals/general-animals/dog-facts
Discover amazing facts about dogs.

INDEX